From Kimchi to Pizza

To My Family, Who Encouraged This Book . . .
. . . and to Fifer and Bodhi, Who Inspired It!

From Kimchi to Pizza
My Little Brother's Adoption Story

**Copyright © 2016 by Margot Horwitz.
All Rights Reserved.**

No part of this publication may be reproduced, stored in a retrieval system or transmitted, in any form or by any means—electronic, mechanical, photocopying, recording or otherwise—without prior written permission from the publisher, except for the inclusion of brief quotations in a review.

For information about this title or to order other books and/or electronic media, contact the publisher: Book Architecture, One Richmond Square, Suite #112K, Providence, RI 02906, www.bookarchitecture.com, email address: author@margothorwitz.com

ISBNs:
hardcover: 978-0-9864204-7-4   softcover: 978-0-9864204-5-0
digital: 978-0-9864204-6-7

Printed in the United States of America
Cover and Interior design: 1106 Design
Editorial: Book Architecture

From Kimchi to Pizza

My Little Brother's Adoption Story

by Margot Horwitz
Illustrations by Dave Stebenne

1

Meeting My New Brother

I remember so clearly the first time I saw the little boy who would soon be my brother, Leo.

He was walking, very slowly, down the hall of the orphanage in Seoul, which is in the country of South Korea. He was holding tightly to the hand of a woman, one of his caregivers. She kept whispering to him, telling him to move more quickly. But Sung (that was his name then) continued taking very small steps until—suddenly—there he was, right in front of me!

Mom and Dad bent down to hug him, and then I went to him. He gave me a little smile. "*Nuna*," he whispered. Then he said it louder. "*Nuna!*" And he put his little arms around me. He only came up to my waist, but he hugged me really tightly.

"That means 'big sister,'" said his caregiver. "He knows who you are, Ruby!"

Mom and Dad stood still as my new brother looked up at them. "*Oma?*" he said to my mother. Then he turned to my father. "*Apa?*" He had been told about them, too.

My parents smiled at him, and then they smiled at me. I bent down to give him a hug of my own. "Hello, Leo Sung!" I said.

He seemed happy to be hugged, but I think he was confused about his name change. I held his hand and tried to explain it to him: "You are Leo Sung. You have a new first name, and your old name will now be your middle name. Like I'm Ruby Megan."

At that moment, a bunch of kids ran over to him, trying to figure out what was going on. Who were these strange people, from another country, who were holding on to their friend? They were very curious, and they chattered away in Korean, which, of course, I could not understand.

"Lei!" said my new brother, pointing to a little girl. My parents and I looked at each other, and we all saw that the girl must be special to him. She went to him, and together they made the peace sign. It was cute, so I took their picture. When I showed them the picture on my camera, they smiled and laughed.

A few minutes later, a man named Johnny came over and told us it was time to go. Johnny was our guide and translator. He was Korean, and I don't think "Johnny" was his Korean name. I think he had another name, just like Leo had another name, Sung.

We followed Johnny, leaving the orphanage. Leo held my hand tightly, and I liked that. He did not look back, and I wondered what he was thinking about.

2
Seeing Seoul With My New Brother

I thought we were going back to the hotel, but my dad told me we were going sightseeing instead. "It will be fun to see Seoul, Ruby!" he said.

I wondered if that would be okay with Leo, but then I remembered that he was still in the city where he had been born. The person who probably felt the most out of place there was me. We saw things I had never seen before, like the changing of the guard, where one group of soldiers replaces

another outside the royal palace. Then Johnny took us to the Museum of Chicken Art. Can you imagine an entire museum where the pictures are all of chickens?

Everything—the smells, the signs, and the style of dress—was different from what we have in the United States, but the food was probably the most different. Of course, we needed to eat, and we had heard about the special donuts at Crown Bakery. But Mom thought we should have some other food before dessert, so we went to a place that served fish steamed with egg and a spicy pickled cabbage called *kimchi*. I couldn't believe I was supposed to eat that stuff! I tried, I really did, but I just couldn't eat it, so the waiter was nice and brought me pasta and red sauce.

It tasted different from the spaghetti at home, but not that different!

Finally, we went to the bakery to have the donuts, and they were as amazing as the people at the orphanage had said.

That night we went to the big market, where there were many stalls and shops that sold anything you could imagine. They even had chocolate-flavored seaweed—no, thank you! They also sold kids' clothes, and Mom and Dad bought each of us a shirt. Leo loved his new shirt. But he got upset when they tried to buy him a new backpack. Dad showed him how this one rolled and had a hard case to keep his things safe.

"I think he wants to keep his old backpack," I said. "I think he wants to hold on to something from his old life."

"That's very smart of you, Ruby," Mom said. "I'll bet you're exactly right. Well, okay, Leo. You can keep your backpack. No problem!"

We saw that Leo was getting tired, so we went back to our hotel. Leo and I played with some toys that we'd brought with us, and I listened to him babble in his own language.

"I think he's going to learn English really fast," said Dad. "We'll just keep talking to him a lot, so he'll get used to the sounds." I sat on the floor near him and talked to him for a little while. I don't think he understood much of what I said, but he seemed happy to have me there.

When it was time for Leo to go to sleep, Mom suggested that we all go to sleep, so that Leo could see what we were doing. It was a little early, but I was tired from all that walking, so I got into bed with Mom, and Leo lay next to Dad.

Suddenly, Leo started to cry. It was as if he was seeing that things were different now, that he was not with his friends and caregivers at the orphanage but instead was with a strange new group of people who looked so different from everyone he knew.

I'm not sure why, but the rest of us, even my Dad, started to cry, too. Leo had touched our hearts. I think they call it empathy, or something like that. For some reason, seeing us cry seemed to make Leo feel better. In a few minutes, he stopped looking so sad, and then he smiled at us. It was sort of like he was thinking, "This is my new family—and they love me!"

3
A Family of Four

A few days later, we got on a plane to go back home. It was really big—there were three sections in one row, with a total of ten seats across. There must have been hundreds and hundreds of people on our plane! I'd flown many times before but never in anything this big. I wasn't sure if Leo had ever even been on a plane before. Dad said he didn't think so.

Leo must have been really tired, because he curled up next to Mom and slept nearly the whole way home. And it was a very long trip—thirteen hours! Dad and I sat together, reading, sleeping, and playing a card game that we made up.

"Dad," I asked, "do you think Leo will play sports?"

"I don't know, Ruby. I have no idea," he said.

"Dad? Will Leo like peanut butter?"

"You mean, like me?"

I kept asking questions like that until an important thought popped into my head.

"Dad, will Leo get into my stuff? Like, my diary?"

"He won't be interested in those things, honey. You'll see. He'll have his own things to play with."

I really hoped Dad was right.

When we finally got back to the United States, we checked into a hotel. (The kid must have thought we had no home, since the only places we had been together were hotels!) Mom gave Leo a bath that night, which was New Year's Eve. Dad texted a photo of "America's newest immigrant" to my grandparents, so they would know we'd gotten back safely. It was Leo's first picture taken in his new country, but I guess he didn't realize that!

4
Settling In

The next day we drove home. It was so amazing that my new brother, so much younger than me, had traveled farther at his age than I ever had before this trip. I thought it was a big deal that I had been to California!

Our life together, as a family of four, had really begun. When we finally got to our house, I took Leo upstairs, to the room we were going to share. "It's just for now," Mom had told me. "Just so he doesn't feel scared on his own. Soon we're going to redo the guest room for you to have as your brand-new room!"

I wasn't so sure about this plan. My parents were usually right, but just to be on the safe side, before going to Seoul, I'd separated all of our toys carefully: I put Leo's stuff on the right side of the room, near the closet, and my things on the left side, behind the bunk bed. That way there would be no mix-ups. I was glad that he had someone to sleep with, but he had to know the rules.

Leo's eyes widened as he looked around the room. He didn't seem to know where to go, so I walked him over to the toys, books, and clothes that our family and friends had sent for him. He looked a little scared. My parents had told me that this was probably more stuff than he had ever had in the orphanage. But when we did a puzzle that was especially for a little boy, he stopped looking scared, and he even smiled.

A few times he wandered over to my side of the room, and each time I guided him back to his side. I tried to explain that I would read the books to him. He got up again and went over to my softball glove. Why was he so much more interested in *my* stuff than his own stuff? Just like I told Dad on the plane!

At least he was happy enough to get into his own bed—the bottom part of the bunk bed. We had been told that it would be a good idea for Leo to have Korean music to listen to while falling asleep. One of his caregivers had given us a CD of the music Leo liked. They are gentle sounds, and we took that CD everywhere with us the first year! The music did seem to help him fall asleep, just as they said it would. (Secretly, I think we all liked the music!)

During the first few weeks, some nights I woke up to find that Leo had climbed up to the top of bunk and was sitting at the edge of my mattress. He was staring at my face, watching me sleep.

"I don't think that's very safe," I said. "Go back to your bed now."

Another thing upset me a little bit: Leo came up to my bed, suddenly, when we had storms with wind, thunder, and lightning. He also sometimes walked into Mom and Dad's

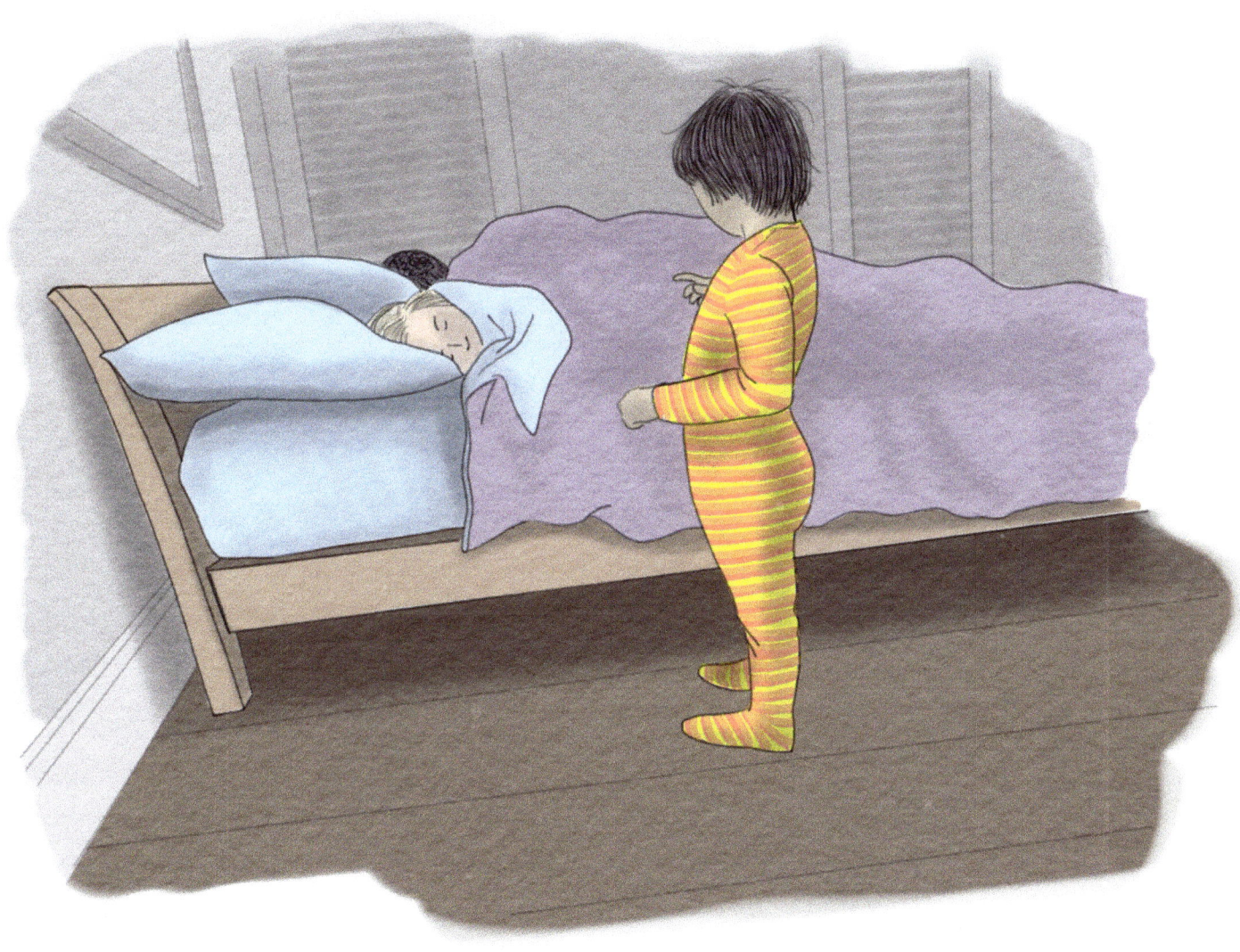

bedroom and stood there, staring at them. I guess he wanted to make sure they were still there.

Whenever I realized Leo was gone, I went to my parents' room and led him back to our room. "Come on, Leo," I would say, reaching for his hand. "You're going to be really tired tomorrow if you don't go back to sleep."

Leo needed rest now, because he had started school.

5
Off to School

All of us knew the best preschool for Leo was the place I had gone, the Williams School. It's the best! The teachers are really nice and helpful, but they make sure everyone behaves.

They were really good to Leo, as a new student from such a different place. They knew that he didn't know a lot of English words at the beginning, but they worked with him until he learned. At first, he had trouble with the alphabet. When he sang the "Alphabet Song," it was sort of funny because he kept saying "l-o-l-o-b" instead of "l-m-n-o-p." But he's smart, and he's picking up English fast.

Something really sweet happened to Leo at Williams. On one of his first days there, he was in the office with a teacher, and he saw a big collage on the wall. It has more than a hundred pictures of kids who have been students at the school, but the teacher told me that he walked right up to my photograph and pointed, saying "Ruby!"

The teachers were so excited that Leo recognized me out of all the kids that they took my picture off the collage and gave it to him to keep in his cubby. That way he would have me with him at school, and it seemed to make him happy.

One day I went with Mom to pick Leo up from school, and all the teachers, who used to be my teachers, made a fuss over me. It was nice to be remembered, and I guess they thought I was a good kid after all!

"Ruby," Mom said to me, "go get Leo from the playground."

There is a playground behind the school. I remembered just where it was.

When I went around the corner, I stopped right away. I couldn't believe what I was seeing: Leo was holding a bat, and one of the teachers was pitching to him. I was happy that he was fitting in and that he wasn't off by himself not playing with anyone. But softball is *my* thing!

I got really upset. "Leo, come on!" I yelled. "It's time to go!" Then I marched back into the office and past Mom to the front door.

"Ruby, honey. What's the matter with you?" Mom asked on our way home.

I didn't tell her. I just went right up to my room. Well, I tried to go to my room, but it's Leo's room, too. Just then, I looked at his stuff and saw that he had taken my "game ball" from my side of the room and put it in his bookcase. The game ball is the one that the coach gives to the player who has played the best that game.

"No, Leo, no!" I yelled at him as I took back my game ball. "Leave my stuff alone!"

Leo went crying to Mom, and I felt sort of bad, but I was still really mad at him.

Later my Dad came up to my room to talk to me.

"What's up, kiddo?"

"I don't want Leo to play softball!"

My Dad laughed, but that just made me even madder.

"It's not funny! Why can't he play soccer? Everyone plays soccer!"

"Honey, he's a really active kid. He'll probably play lots of sports!"

"Okay, that's fine. But no softball. You have to promise!"

My Dad looked at me as if he couldn't tell whether I was serious.

"Okay, Ruby. We won't sign him up for softball. I promise."

"And he can't have a hamster!

(I have a brown and white hamster whose name is Amos Maxwell Fuzzington.)

"Okay, Ruby. No softball and no hamster."

I felt better, and Dad kissed me on the head before he left. At the door to my room, he stopped. "You know, Ruby Megan, one day you'll realize that Leo wanting to do the things you do is the highest compliment he could ever give you. I know right now it's annoying, but one day you'll know what I'm talking about."

6
Growing Up, Together

Well, that day didn't come, I can tell you! Leo got to do almost everything he wanted—he even got his own hamster—but I got to keep softball as my own thing.

Leo grew really fast. One day he was racing trucks up and down the hall, and the next day (so it seemed) he won his class's Halloween art contest. He began to have a life of his own and made friends at school who came over to our house to play.

It was good that I finally moved into my own room, because then he had his own place to be with his friends. It was nice to have only my clothes in the closet and my books in the bookcases. I got to decorate my room exactly the way I wanted, with fancy black-and-white pictures from Europe. I guess Leo wasn't the only one growing up.

Now that Leo could talk English, he talked all the time! That was good and bad, because there was absolutely no silence, and that can be annoying. When I wanted to tease him, I reminded him of when he used to sing "l-o-l-o-b." That wasn't really making fun of him—he was so much older by then that it didn't matter.

Yesterday, for example, he said something really interesting to me.

"When it's raining, that's because God's crying, Ruby. And when it's thundering, that's because he's mad. And when he's happy, that's a sunny day like this. And when he's really happy, that's a rainbow!"

"Wow, Leo! Okay!"

Times like that, when Leo said interesting things, I could see that he was comfortable talking to me and that he felt a part of the family. That seems really important. Because he's adopted, we have to make sure that he knows we love him and are here to take good care of him.

Of course, as a member of the family, he had some jobs to do—though I still had more than he did! I think he began to understand that everyone has to help out. I guess that's another way of making him feel that he belongs.

7
On the Same Team

That year, my softball team went to the league championship. It was so exciting! We had been good before, but we had never been that good. I played second base and usually batted second, except for sometimes when I batted fifth.

In the semifinal game, our pitcher, Laura—who is our best player—hit a ball so far I couldn't believe it! She rounded the bases, trying to score an important run that would have put our team ahead for good. But when she slid into home plate, she hurt her knee. She was really in pain, although she tried not to cry.

The coach said that she was going to be fine, in time, but that she wouldn't be able to pitch in the championship game.

"Ruby," he said to me, "you're going to have to pitch for us. Okay?"

"What?" I almost screamed. "No! I can't do that! This is the biggest game of the year!"

"But you're our second-best pitcher, Ruby. You'll be fine. It's just like when Laura was away visiting her grandparents."

I tried to be a good sport about it, but I was so nervous

inside. It wouldn't be the same as when Laura had been away. That was just a regular-season game.

On the day of the championship game, I couldn't talk to anybody. When we got to the field, the members of the other team, the Dragons, all seemed bigger than us. They were wearing dark green, and we were wearing royal blue, because we were the Royals. We were playing at the Dragons' home field, so a lot of the people in the stands were their family and friends.

Mom went to the stands and waved at me, but I was too nervous to wave back. She had Leo with her, and my Dad was going to come from work before the game was half over.

I pitched pretty badly in the first inning: I walked three

people, and one girl got a hit, so the Dragons were ahead 2–0. In the next inning, we scored one run, but they scored another two, so then we were down by three, 4–1.

Coach came over to me when I got to the dugout. "Hey, Ruby. Don't worry, kid! It's just a game. Okay, kid?"

He patted me on the leg and went out to coach first base, because our team was up at bat.

Of course I'd heard "It's just a game" many times before, but this time it seemed to sink in. I started to think about all of the hard things in life, like when my friend Angela had to go to the hospital to have her appendix taken out. I would have been so scared if I had been her, but she was really brave.

Then, for some reason, I thought about Leo. I pictured him walking out of the orphanage and not looking back. He must have been scared then, and he cried the first night at the hotel, but now he was telling me that when God was "really happy, well, that's a rainbow!"

"Hey, Leo!" I called suddenly through the metal fence. "Leo! Come here a minute!"

Mom stood up and could see that I was waving, so she sent Leo to me. When he got to the door in the metal gate, I opened it and let him into the dugout.

"Now, listen. You see that girl who's up at bat? If she gets a hit, she's going to leave her bat there. I want you to run out and get her bat and bring it back here. Coach, is it okay if my brother, Leo, is our bat boy?!"

"Sure thing!" Coach called back. "Glad to have you, Leo kid!"

I was glad Coach said that, because it made Leo feel a part of the team. I thought of the times when we go out to a restaurant or some other public place. Sometimes people look at Leo, wondering if he is part of our family, since he looks so different from the rest of us. Those times I feel really protective of him—of course he's a member of our family!

Leo was so happy to be in the dugout that he stayed there the whole game. Having him near me wasn't annoying. In fact, for some reason, I started to pitch better. We kept scoring one run each inning, but because I didn't give up any more runs, we ended up winning 5–4!

Our whole team was so excited! We tried not to be rude to the other team, but later when we were in the pizza parlor we were really happy. Leo and Dad went with us. Mom had offered to take Leo home so that I could celebrate with my team, but I said, "No. He has to be with us! Leo is our bat boy now! We wouldn't have won without him!" Leo looked so happy, and he ate a big slice of pizza.

These days I'm feeling really good about Leo being part of our family. I think he feels good about it, too. Before he went to bed on the night of the big game, he asked me to tuck him in. (Usually he likes Mom or Dad to do it, but this time he asked me.) As he was falling asleep, he told me that it had been "the favorite day of my whole life."

"Me too, Leo," I whispered. "Me too!"

www.ingramcontent.com/pod-product-compliance
Lightning Source LLC
Chambersburg PA
CBHW061120010526
44112CB00024B/2926